1

You Can Tell
You're a Midwesterner
When . . . .

by
Dale Grooms

QUIXOTE PRESS
1854-345th Avenue
Wever IA
52658
1-800-571-2665

QUIXOTE PRESS
Bruce Carlson
1854-345th Avenue
Wever IA 52658

DEDICATION

I dedicate this book to my folks, Harold and Wanda Grooms, for raising me in the most Midwestern of ways.

To my lovely wife, Becky Grooms, for smoothing my rough edges.

To my son Tyler Grooms, for reminding us to laugh at ourselves.

To all those Midwestern "straight-shooters" out there, that say what they mean and mean what they say.

you're not necessarily
"notorious" nor "famous"
but everyone in the county
knows who you are anyway."

. . your schools have gangs and
they wear their colors,
usually green, and that's
for John Deere."

. . You're so set in your
ways that you don't understand "modern con-
veniences". One fella
thought that the microwave his son
gave him was a breadbox with a
light in it.

. . you're broke, so
you turn cans in
for cash."

. . You gotta have gravy
with every meal."

. . you can adapt to all weather changes because every hour you havta."

. . you realize there's the same number of churches and bars in the town."

. . you like any band that can play a good polka."

. . you believe in two
basic food groups,
meat and potatos."

. . you have two sets
of rosy cheeks."

. . you plant your old
machinery and call
it art."

. . you tell your kids, "I had to walk five miles to get to school."

. . you define a yuppie as a person that buys a new tractor and pickup in the same year."

. . a drive-by shooting means you scared away some out-of-state hunters."

. . you know your taxes
are going up regardless
if your crops do."

. . you believe in the
work ethic, a full day's
work for a half-a-day's
pay."

. . you understand because
you have walked in the
other fellow's shoes. You
had too. With brothers and
sisters, all you got was
hand me downs."

. . you can get your
choice of several
horses or cows if ya
willin' to marry one of
the farmers' daughters
that has reached
legal age."

. . relaxation techniques
called "yoga" in the east
are called "naps" by
you."

. . you don't talk bad
about your neighbors
because there's a good
chance you're related
to them."

. . you don't know beans
about IRA's and 401K's
but you know about
22's and 357's.

. . the men don't know
their wedding anniversary
date but they know all
of the hunting seasons."

. . Ya have no hidden
"political agenda."
We pray. We work.
We starve.

. . ya put your address
numbers in reverse order
on your house just to
see if anyone will
even notice."

. . ya like town hall meetings
because your small town
vote really counts."

. .ya know the names
everyone's pets in
the county."

. . ya fish, swim, hunt and ice skate off of the same farm pond."

. . ya think that "central air conditioning" means leaving all the windows open."

. . ya figure you're a tough guy because you can tear the local small town phone book in half."

. . ya favorite sport is eight man football and your brothers and sisters makes up half the team."

. . ya know the make and color of every fella's vehicle in the county."

FUTHERMORE.
. . ya understand that a new car is one that is less than a decade old."

. . ya never can seem to remember to lock anything up and luckily, it does'nt seem to matter anyway."

. . ya spend as much time raising the neighbor kids as ya do your own kids."

. . ya measure a person's
ego by the size of
buckle they wear."

. . ya reminisce bout the
"good ole days" when ya
got paid for plantin'
insteada not plantin'."

. . ya can't get a
bank loan cause the
banks tell ya, "You
gotta have money in
order to borrow it."

. . . ya don't believe in "carnival rides".
Ya get the same effect acceleratin
over hilly gravel roads."

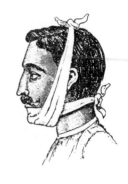

. . You go to the
"county fair's
parade and the
winnin' "float"
is the fire truck.

. . ya ain't got runnin'
water or natural gas
but ya gotta "satellite
dish" in the backyard."

. . ya know that the
railroad tracks splits
the town in two. Ya
have the poverty side,
and the near poverty
side."

. . you know "honesty" is a
given. You go to the
used car lot and the
salesman talks you
out of buyin the car."

. . you know where to find
the town's "grafitti",
On the water tower and under
the bridge. Ya recognize the names
written there."

. . you ain't surprised
that the local milk
cartons have pictures of
"missin' pets" on the
back sides."

. . Ya know that ya don't
havta be AWOL for three
days to be considered
"missin". If ya ain't
found at the local coffee
shop, then foul play is
suspected."

. . ya know what it feels
like to take a whiz
on an electric
fence."

. . ya guesstimate your
town's population of
kids by drivin' down
every street. Countin'
all cats, dogs and
bikes and dividin'
by three."

. . ya carry around credit
cards just fer good looks.
Ya smart enough not to
use 'em."

. . you realize somethin'
is broke when you can't
jimmee rig it with
pliers and wires.

. . you can recognize any
particular species of
road kill for better than
a 100 yards away."

. . you were born in
February and you still
turned out to be the first
New Year's baby of
the town."

. . ya know why the small town noon whistle is always wrong. The whistle blower sets his watch by the clock in the drugstore. The druggist sets his clock by the noon whistle."

. . ya think "multi-culturism" refers to eating at several restaurants that don't serve meat and potatos."

. . ya have a crime happen in the neighborhood and everyone suspects the same couple of people."

. . you're convinced that All-Star Wrestling is real."

. . you expect the local paper to print the weather predictions on the opinion page."

. . you absolutely refuse to pay for anything that you can do yourself."

. . you gotta thermometer on your house and a rain guage on the fence. Ya still think a meteorologist is a fella concerned about large rocks striking the earth."

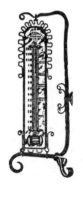

. . ya think the war on drugs means that every county hires a fella to keep the ditch weed mowed. This keeps the young folk from smokin it."

. . ya ain't surprised that your small town doctor is still makin housecalls."

. . ya figure that you'll get invited to nearly every party in town."

. . ya ride faster on gravel roads than the truckers drive on the interstate."

. . ya think "Aids" was somethin your churchs was a collectin' for the homeless people."

. . ya tend to be a "defensive driver
The expert in the backseat tends to
make ya mighty defensive.

George, I told ya to turn right,
how fast are ya goin anyway?"

. . ya still bend over to pick
change off of the ground.

. . Is that a nickel?

. . ya only worry about one precious
metal, and that's Mercury.

. . ya realize that if Jack Frost
comes to early, then once again
you won't have Jack . ."

. . ya notice that the tallest building in the county seat is the "grain elevator"."

. . ya borrow the town's tennis court net on occassion,

. . ya sure like to get your limit of fish at the river."

. . ya pretty easy going. The only time you have an axe to grind, is when it's time to split wood again.

. . ya "standard of living" is relative. It's relative to the genorosity of your relatives."

CORN COB

. . Ya have at least 101 uses for a corncob, but only one practical use in an outdoor emergency."

. . ya realize that the "new" and "improved" printed on items at the supermarket is only describing the package and not the product."

ya also realize that the "new" and "improved" must be describin' the supermarket's profits lately."

. . you still prefer
five and dime stores
over malls.
BESIDES, ya get
more for your
money."

. . you realize that second
hand stores are now big
business.

. . you like your second
hand stores almost as
well as the five and
dime stores."

. . you encourage your kids to
enlist in the military, so
they can start eatin three
meals a day."

BESIDES. . Their grandpa
starts every conversation with
"After the war . . ."
Maybe they will eventually be
able to communicate with
grandpa."

. . ya gotta "welcome" mat
by the front door and
yer sincere about it."

. . ya gotta old
tool shed, but
tools are the last
thing you will find
in there."

. . you realize
that it's an
acceptable absense
for kids to miss several
days of school durin
the plantin season."

34

. . you define a "hidden investment" as a twenty dollar bill stuck between two mattresses."

. . you realize there's only two types of job listings; part-time permanent and full-time temporary."

. . ya still donate plasma for benevolent reasons rather than financial reasons."

. . ya realize that a new car now costs the same amount that you paid for your first house."

. . ya realize that creative financing is a fancy word for gettin a loan to pay off a loan to pay off another loan."

. . you a good employee cause you get lots of practice simultaneously holding down two different jobs."

. . ya kids would ride their horses to school but it's against some ordinance."

. . yer grandkids
really love you.
They remember to
tell ya that, right
before Christmas
and Easter."

. . ya don't believe in fancy
architecture, cause ya believe
function is more important
than form. ya spouse believes
in function before form too.
It's a good thing, otherwise
ya both would still be
single."

. . you realize we don't "social events" out here, we have "feedin" events. The most popular ones are; pancake, watermelon, spaghetti and chili feeds."

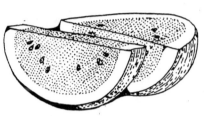

. . ya don't need Keno or Powerball. It's enough excitement to roll the dice and see who's buyin' lunch."

. . ya know that ya don't havta wait til the 4th of July to see an air show. Ya can watch the locos that do their own crop dustin."

. . ya glad there's still
plenty of old timers that
have junk yards. At least
ya can get parts for yer
ole motorized
contraptions."

. . ya know parents can
easily find the kids,
just follow the trail
of clothes."

. . ya know dinner is served at noon, lunch is a midafternoon snack and supper is the evening meal. The folks at the coast mistake dinner for supper and they tend to eat when they should be sleepin."

. . you not a finatical exerciser" but when you hear the local tornado siren you're off and runnin."

SUGARPLUM

. . ya gotta "nickname"
for most of yer friends and
they have several pretty
accurate nicknames for you
too."

. . ya realize that
wearin "long john underwear"
in the winter is not a fashion
statement,
it's a necessity."

. . ya could win the lottery
tommorrow and ya
would still clock into
work the next
day."

. . ya realize that a full
service barbershop is
one that trims ya
hair nostrils too."

. . ya notice the wives
practicin cuttin hair on
their kids. If they make a
few mistakes then the kids
are right in style with
the kids from the coast."

. . ya thought a "bilingual" was a fella
that could speak at least 2 dialects of
Midwestern talk.

. . it takes ya hours to
finish a checkers game
cause ya keep forgettin
who's got the next
move."

. . ya realize that yer in trouble regardless of ya age when people are usin your middle name loudly with that shrill accent on the last syllable."

. . ya have a favorite chair and ya better believe that nobody sits in it accept you."

. . ya do ya best thinkin on ya "favorite chair". and ya do most of that thinkin before and after work."

. . ya realize the reason
that fellas so freely
trade seed caps. It's so
windy

. . ya can identify dozens
of weeds and thistles
usually by the age of
four."

. . ya don't need any compasses
out here. Midwesterners
naturally have a sense of
direction about them and
they rarely head East."

. . ya realize the difficulty of anonymously reporting crimes in these small midwestern towns. The person receiving your phone message will recognize ya voice."

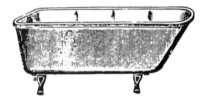

. . ya use the ole bathtub to store ya live fishin bait in the backyard. The kids find out who's the bravest, tryin to catch crawdads with their bare hands."

. . ya "ring finger grows a couple of sizes in the winter and settles back down in the summer. it ain't nearly as volitole as ya stomach."

. . ya finance ya
annual family vacations by saving
yer change in empty quart canning
jars. Ya fill one jar for
every hundred miles ya plan
to travel."

. . ya like ya dependable
clothes dryer with
the life time
guarantee. It's
called "the great
outdoors."

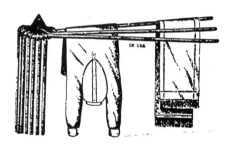

. . ya own several pieces
of "fine china" but it's
against house rules to
eat off of them."

. . ya actually store medicines in the medicine cabinet and gloves in the glove box, but door knobs seem to work best for hangin ya ole work clothes."

. . ya don't need a pot of grease to have a "fondue party". Ya stick ya hotdogs into the campfire."

. . ya know the junk dealer ain't really a junk dealer unless he's located near the railroad tracks."

. . ya family prefers to "rough it" when they go campin. They ain't about to pitch a tent somewhere that charges ya money to do that."

. . ya know that "ridin high in the saddle" means ya just got paid."

. . ya have been fishin enough times to know the bigger the hook ya use, the bigger the snag ya catch."

. . ya recognize when grandpa is losin his sight. He reaches into his pocket to give the grandkids some change and he hands them washers."

. . ya never under estimate the power of a "bake sale"; be it pies, cookies, brownies or otherwise. Most all home makers out here moonlight as home bakers."

. . ya ain't surprised when men let their wives cut their hair, but out here men prefer payin the barber for a clean shave."

. . ya have no need for "clay pigeons" durin target practice. Ya prefer the more difficult challenge of shootin actual pigeons as they fly off of the barn."

. . ya kids' inheritances don't require lawyers. The oldest boy gets grandpa's shotgun and the oldest girl gets grandma's quilts."

. . ya used to "no frills" funerals. Out here, folks choose the economical plywood casket, or they can choose the deluxe double plywood casket."

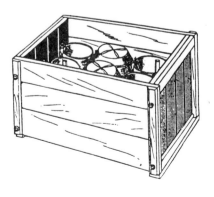

. . ya realize that
it does'nt havta be
the 4th of July for
yer town to have a
dance in the middle
of main street,
but ya can bet
that it's a
Saturday nite."

. . ya bedroon is a
mess but yer sleepin
under "award winnin"
quilts that earned
recognition at the
County Fair."

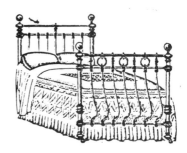

. . ya notice that men only need
one mug out here. they use one
of those universal types, the
kind that holds coffee and beer."

. . ya knew what "heartland" music was before Garth Brooks introduced it."

. . ya notice that yer hand operated kitchen utensils tend to outlast the electric ones."

. . ya got ya kids "conditioned". When ya ring the cowbell on the front porch they come runnin' home for supper."

. . ya make sure all of yer socks are the same color. That way, they almost match."

. . ya know "fencin" ain't a sportin event, it's to keep the cows in and the varmints out."

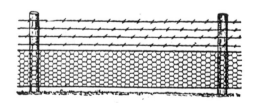

. . ya wear a suit on a week day and yer friends want to know "what wedding or funeral are ya attendin?"

. . ya have no apptitude for being a good sales person. Ya too good at sayin' what ya meanin' and meanin' what ya sayin'."

. . ya recognize the fact that yer a part of nature cause that is yer nature."

. . ya find "motels" confusin. They tend to wrap things around cups and toilet seats as if they don't want ya usen em."

. . yer idea of "campin" is to cook marshmellows and hotdogs over the wood stove."

. . ya still have the bible that ya earned from graduating from ya eighth grade church confirmation class."

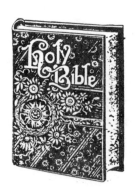

. . ya notice the women are doin 90% of the housework. Men are willin to help, its just the fact that some things gotta be done right."

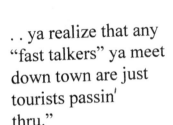

. . ya realize that any "fast talkers" ya meet down town are just tourists passin' thru."

. . ya suspect that a "vegetarian" is a person that recently had to sell all of their cattle for financial reasons."

. . . you can't carry much of a tune, but neither can anyone else, so ya forced to sing loudly.

. . . ya small town church needs everyone in the choir, so the men attempt to sing monotone and the women give soprano their best shot."

. . . ya prefer driving vehicles and other motorized contraptions that are at least 20 years old. That way, ya can tune em up with a screwdriver cause modern technology has'nt ruined em yet."

. . . you never get "insomia" cause yer chores start at sun rise leavin ya little time fer the occasion."

. . . ya notice they don't put up orange barrels at construction and road sites out here. Too many people think they are supposed to practice ridin' their horses around them."

. . . you're so "stubborn" that when the coroner pronounces you dead, you march outta there to get a second opinion."

. . . ya remember when newspapers used
to separate the fiction, gossip and news sections."

. . . you realize it's easy to stock the
local museums. Ya can dig up arrowheads
and dinosaur bones in yer own backyard."

. . . your idea of shopping
is to find it at a
garage sale or auction
house, or else you don't
need it."

. . . you found out the hard way that it's not a good idea to defrost yer windshield with a pan of hot water."

. . . you realize the "divorce rate" is still low out here cause most of us can't afford caller I.D."

. . . the people living on "welfare" seem to have the same standard of living as you. There's certainly not much difference in those wooden houses we live in."

. . . yer ole clothes are back in style but ya never stopped wearin 'em in the first place."

. . . you really watch yer manners around the evening supper table. If ya don't, you realize that you will be doin' the dishes."

. . . you're quite a character. It's no wonder. "Perseverence" develops character, and lord knows, you can't make it in this country without it."

. . . you get depressed when your favorite team loses two games in a row."

. . . ya got a built in "snooze alarm'. When the newspaper hits the front screen door ya know it's really time to get up."

430 . . . you have no problems buyin gifts for "ole timers". Ya realize that an ole John Wayne movie or an ole Johny Cash tape will suite em just fine."

. . . ya never thought you'd see the day, when parents are now startin to obey their children."

. . . you rarely leave the county unless there's a state rodeo, fair or state sportin event finals goin on.

. . . ya used to gettin a 40% discount on ya meat, dairy and poultry purchases. Ya buy direct. Ya buy directly from the farmer."

. . . ya know how many "bachelorettes" are in town. Ya drive by the local "honky-tonk" on Saturday night, count the number of fellas dukin' it out and divide by two."

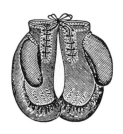

. . . ya think of "future shock"
as the time ya reach retirement age
but yer not drawin' a retirement wage."

. . . ya don't gossip cause ya
realize anyone can go to the
"coffeeshop" and find out who
started the gossip in the first place."

. . . all the presents from the kids
er still in the packages cuz they're
jest too perty to use.

"All aah laak ta dews write music."

. . . you make sure that yer occupation ain't so important as to need a briefcase.

. . . ya realize there's lots of "romantics" out here cause marryin' fer money ain't hardly possible."

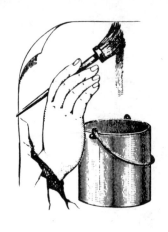

. . . you notice that nobody
paints their houses red out here,
it will be mistaken for a barn."

. . . you know when spring is here.
That's when everyone starts to take
down their Christmas lites in front
of the house."

. . . ya ain't a draft dodger. Most
folks out here get excited about their
first trip outside the county."

. . . you save yer "horn blowers" from the New Year's parties cause ya discovered they work as "duck calls".

. . . you treat all people with great respect cause what comes around goes around. In this sparse country it's known as the "boomerang effect".

. . . ya ain't a "psychologist" but ya
realize that a simple life style keeps
the therapist away."

. . . you nitice that the "modern
art" along the interstate sure looks
like "farm equipment" that was
recently struck by a Midwest twister."

... ya know how to spot the town liar. That's the person that always gets an inch more rain in his rain guage than everybody else."

... you use the BFH (big farmin hammer) to fix anything that's bein stubborn. If ya can't fix it, at least ya can break it in style.

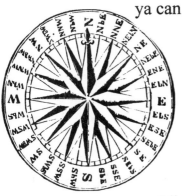

... ya never have trouble given "directions" to strangers in rural areas, cause the telephone poles are numbered so we can use 'em as road markers."

. . . you realize "spring trainin" starts first thing after winter. Ya gotta drop 20 lbs. quick in order to fit into yer summer clothes or else buy a new wardrobe."

. . . ya understand the "Bill of Rights" but realize ya waive those rights once ya take yer "weddin vows."

. . . ya got several "snooze alarms" on a Sunday morning. First it's the newspaper, then, ya hear the teenagers tryin' to sneak back into the house.

. . . you generally go on an annual diet, out here we call it "Lent".

. . . you never get "gaudy" or "giddy"
cause out here yer expected to "walk the talk".

. . . ya a "jack of all
trades" cause ya never
stopped using the
barter system. Horse-
tradin' is a big part
of life out here."

. . . yer "grunts" have significant
meaning. "Aha" means ya finally
understan'. "Ahm" means yer
passin negative judgement on
somebody."

. . . you take care of each others'
"achy-breaky" hearts."

. . . you realize that not only are
you tithing with the church
but with the state and
Federal Government as well.

YESSIREE:

. . . you really watch yer manners around the evening
supper table. If ya don't, you realize that you
will be doin' the dishes."

. . . ya notice that the local newspapers don't carry any world news. It tends to be a bad influence on us.

. . . you also notice that the new job openings are mathematically related to the new listins in the obituary column."

. . . ya observations also tell ya, that those newspaper boys keep gettin older and older.

February

. . . you used to "February" bein' the most difficult month to spell, pronounce and get thru. In fact, the best way to weather February is to think of May.

. . . ya don't havta invest in fertilizer for yer garden. Ya got the real stuff right close to home."

. . . you notice folks like to help in emergencies out here cause there's a good chance the sheriff will deputize 'em. That's a real honor out here."

. . . you realize that "boatin accidents" can be serious out here. Ya never know when yer goin' to hit a sandbar."

. . . yer not to friendly at auctions. If ya wave at all yer friends ya realize you'll end up buyin the place."

. . you give yer babies "rattlers" to play with buy ya make sure the rest of the snake is'nt still connected."

. . . yer usually independent buy ya get mighty "dependent" come April 15th."

. . . "ya realize that all this
"down-sizing would'nt be needed
if companies stopped hiring
consultants to come up with
these ideas."

. . . ya remember winnin' "carnival
glass" at the fair by throwin nickels,
now, the antique shops got tourists lined
up throwin twenty dollar bills for em."

. . . ya realize ya don't need
"marriage counselors or "financial
advisers" out here. Mother in Laws
will take care of those services
free of charge."

. . . you consider yer "iron skillets" to be precious metals cause food cooked outta those skillets tastes as good as gold."

. . . ya say yer goin' "downtown" even though yer town sits atop a hill."

. . . you figure yer "furniture ain't brokin' in yet, if ya haven't at least repaired it once with plywood."

. . . you realize there's still "desperados" out here, but we call em out of state deer hunters."

. . . ya all head for grandma's for lunch right after church. Nobody's cookin' ever come close to measurin' up to grandma's."

. . . you realize that some of the pets out here are more "housebroken" than some of the husbands."

. . . you realize that when a cop asks ya for "proof of car insurance" that out here, ya just open yer car trunk and show em yer spare battery, spare tire and yer jumper cables."

. . . ya notice the men have their clothes layin' around the house but all their tools are neatly organized in the garage."

. . . ya don't save money
for a rainy day, ya save money
in case it don't rain."

. . . ya know the only sure fire crop
around here seems to be "raisin kids".

. . . you realize a limited vocabulary is acceptable out here. Most communications are done by hand gestures, cap movements and facial expressions any way."

. . . ya vote regularly and ya take particular interest to ignore the particular interests of the special interest groups."

. . . ya figured "arrears" referred to a catch-all accounting term, as, "we are all up to our ears in debt come April 15."

. . . you notice that the schools only send the tall kids on "field trips". The shorter kids ain't much help at detasseling corn."

. . . ya kids display their
"masterpieces" on the fridge
held up with fruit magnets."

. . . you realize people are
so reasonable out here that most
differences are settled with the
flip of a coin. If yer battin' 50%
in this country, that ain't all bad."

. . . you realize "flophouses"
still exist out here but ya gotta
find yer own date."

. . . ya don't over-do hair spray or smell-good stuff cause it tends to attract mosquitoes and wasps."

. . . you know the watermelon theives. Their the fellas with lots of stitches under their britches."

. . . yer proud of yer "heritage" cause Jesus told the farmin' people years ago that "the poor shall be rich".

. . . ya no scholar but ya "self-educated" about the models and parts of cars and trucks built in the last twenty years."

. . . ya have breakfast for supper you know that means that the hens laid too many eggs."

. . . you notice that despite Lent everybody is a little heavy out here except for 'bankers'. Not only do they look "lean" they usually hold one against ya as well."

. . . ya know the most effective
place to plant yer garden is right close
to the horse tank and wind mill."

. . . ya define "landscapin" as
makin the most outta railroad
ties and wagon wheels around
the outside of yer house."

Please send me ___copies at $7.95 each.
(Make checks payable to **QUIXOTE PRESS**.)

Name _____

Street _____

City _____

SEND ORDER TO:
QUIXOTE PRESS
1854-345 Avenue
Wever IA 52658
1-800-571-2665

Since you have enjoyed this book, perhaps you would be interest in some of these others from QUIXOTE PRESS.

ARKANSAS BOOKS

ARKANSAS' ROADKILL COOKBOOK
  by Bruce Carlson ....paperback $7.95
REVENGE OF ROADKILL
  by Bruce Carlson ....paperback $7.95
LET'S US GO DOWN TO THE RIVER 'N...
  by Various Authors ....paperback $9.95
TALL TALES OF THE MISSISSIPPI RIVER
  by Dan Titus ....paperback $9.95
LOST & BURIED TREASURE OF THE MISSISSIPPI RIVER
  by Netha Bell & Gary Scholl ....paperback $9.95
TALES OF HACKETT'S CREEK
  by Dan Titus ....paperback $9.95
101 WAYS TO USE A DEAD RIVER FLY
  by Bruce Carlson ....paperback $7.95
VACANT LOT, SCHOOL YARD & BACK ALLEY GAMES
  by Various Authors ....paperback $9.95
HOW TO TALK MIDWESTERN
  by Robert Thomas ....paperback $7.95
ARKANSAS COOKIN'
  by Bruce Carlson ....(3x5) paperback $5.95

DAKOTA BOOKS

HOW TO TALK DAKOTA ....paperback $7.95
Some Pretty Tame, but Kinda Funny Stories About Early
DAKOTA LADIES-OF-THE-EVENING
  by Bruce Carlson ....paperback $9.95
SOUTH DAKOTA ROADKILL COOKBOOK
  by Bruce Carlson ....paperback $7.95

REVENGE OF ROADKILL
by Bruce Carlson ....paperback $7.95
101 WAYS TO USE A DEAD RIVER FLY
by Bruce Carlson ....paperback $7.95
LET'S US GO DOWN TO THE RIVER 'N...
by Various Authors ....paperback $9.95
LOST & BURIED TREASURE OF THE MISSOURI RIVER
by Netha Bell ....paperback $9.95
MAKIN' DO IN SOUTH DAKOTA
by Various Authors ....paperback $9.95
THE DAKOTAS' VANSHING OUTHOUSE
by Bruce Carlson ....paperback $9.95
VACANT LOT, SCHOOL YARD & BACK ALLEY GAMES
by Various Authors ....paperback $9.95
HOW TO TALK MIDWESTERN
by Robert Thomas ....paperback $7.95
DAKOTA COOKIN'
by Bruce Carlson ....(3x5) paperback $5.95

ILLINOIS BOOKS

ILLINOIS COOKIN'
by Bruce Carlson ....(3x5) paperback $5.95
THE VANISHING OUTHOUSE OF ILLINOIS
by Bruce Carlson ....paperback $9.95
A FIELD GUIDE TO ILLINOIS' CRITTERS
by Bruce Carlson ....paperback $7.95
Some Pretty Tame, but Kinda Funny Stories About Early
ILLINOIS LADIES-OF-THE-EVENING
by Bruce Carlson ....paperback $9.95

ILLINOIS' ROADKILL COOKBOOK
by Bruce Carlson ....paperback $7.95
101 WAYS TO USE A DEAD RIVER FLY
by Bruce Carlson ....paperback $7.95
HOW TO TALK ILLINOIS
by Netha Bell ....paperback $7.95
TALL TALES OF THE MISSISSIPPI RIVER
by Dan Titus ....paperback $9.95
TALES OF HACKETT'S CREEK
by Dan Titus ....paperback $9.95
LOST & BURIED TREASURE OF THE MISSISSIPPI RIVER
by Netha Bell & Gary Scholl ....paperback $9.95
STRANGE FOLKS ALONG THE MISSISSIPPI
by Pat Wallace ....paperback $9.95
LET'S US GO DOWN TO THE RIVER 'N...
by Various Authors ....paperback $9.95
MISSISSIPPI RIVER PO' FOLK
by Pat Wallace ....paperback $9.95
GHOSTS OF THE MISSISSIPPI RIVER
(from Keokuk to St. Louis)
by Bruce Carlson ....paperback $9.95
GHOSTS OF THE MISSISSIPPI RIVER
(from Dubuque to Keokuk)
by Bruce Carlson ....paperback $9.95
MAKIN' DO IN ILLINOIS
by Various Authors ....paperback $9.95
MY VERY FIRST
by Various Authors ....paperback $9.95
VACANT LOT, SCHOOL YARD & BACK ALLEY GAMES
by Various Authors ....paperback $9.95
HOW TO TALK MIDWESTERN
by Robert Thomas ....paperback $7.95

INDIANA BOOKS

REVENGE OF ROADKILL
　　　　　by Bruce Carlson ....paperback $7.95
LET'S US GO DOWN TO THE RIVER 'N...
　　　　　by Various Authors ....paperback $9.95
101 WAYS TO USE A DEAD RIVER FLY
　　　　　by Bruce Carlson ....paperback $7.95
VACANT LOT, SCHOOL YARD & BACK ALLEY GAMES
　　　　　by Various Authors ....paperback $9.95
HOW TO TALK MIDWESTERN
　　　　　by Robert Thomas ....paperback $7.95
INDIANA PRAIRIE SKIRTS
　　　　　by Bev Faaborg & Lois Brinkman .....paperback $9.95
INDIANA COOKIN'
　　　　　by Bruce Carlson ....(3x5) paperback $5.95

IOWA BOOKS

IOWA COOKIN'
　　　　　by Bruce Carlson ....(3x5) paperback $5.95
IOWA'S ROADKILL COOKBOOK
　　　　　by Bruce Carlson ....paperback $7.95
REVENGE OF ROADKILL
　　　　　by Bruce Carlson ....paperback $7.95
GHOSTS OF THE AMANA COLONIES
　　　　　by Lori Erickson ....paperback $9.95
GHOSTS OF THE IOWA GREAT LAKES
　　　　　by Bruce Carlson ....paperback $9.95
GHOSTS OF THE MISSISSIPPI RIVER
(from Dubuque to Keokuk)
　　　　　by Bruce Carlson ....paperback $9.95

GHOSTS OF THE MISSISSIPPI RIVER
(from Minneapolis to Dubuque)
　　　　by Bruce Carlson ....paperback $9.95
GHOSTS OF POLK COUNTY, IOWA
　　　　by Tom Welch ....paperback $9.95
TALES OF HACKETT'S CREEK
　　　　by Dan Titus ....paperback $9.95
TALL TALES OF THE MISSISSIPPI RIVER
　　　　by Dan Titus ....paperback $9.95
101 WAYS TO USE A DEAD RIVER FLY
　　　　by Bruce Carlson ....paperback $7.95
LET'S US GO DOWN TO THE RIVER 'N...
　　　　by Various Authors ....paperback $9.95
TRICKS WE PLAYED IN IOWA
　　　　by Various Authors ....paperback $9.95
IOWA, THE LAND BETWEEN THE VOWELS
(farm boy stories from the early 1900s)
　　　　by Bruce Carlson ....paperback $9.95
LOST & BURIED TREASURE OF THE MISSISSIPPI RIVER
　　　　by Netha Bell & Gary Scholl ....paperback $9.95
Some Pretty Tame, but Kinda Funny Stories About Early
IOWA LADIES-OF-THE-EVENING
　　　　by Bruce Carlson ....paperback $9.95
THE VANISHING OUTHOUSE OF IOWA
　　　　by Bruce Carlson ....paperback $9.95
IOWA'S EARLY HOME REMEDIES
　　　　by 26 Students at Wapello Elem. School ..paperback $9.95
IOWA - A JOURNEY IN A PROMISED LAND
　　　　by Kathy Yoder ....paperback $16.95
LOST & BURIED TREASURE OF THE MISSOURI RIVER
　　　　by Netha Bell ....paperback $9.95
FIELD GUIDE TO IOWA'S CRITTERS
　　　　by Bruce Carlson ....paperback $7.95
OLD IOWA HOUSES, YOUNG LOVES
　　　　by Bruce Carlson ....paperback $9.95

SKUNK RIVER ANTHOLOGY
        by Gene Olson . . . . .paperback $9.95
VACANT LOT, SCHOOL YARD & BACK ALLEY GAMES
        by Various Authors . . . . .paperback $9.95
HOW TO TALK MIDWESTERN
        by Robert Thomas . . . . .paperback $7.95

KANSAS BOOKS

HOW TO TALK KANSAS . . . . .paperback $7.95
STOPOVER IN KANSAS
        by Jon McAlpin . . . . .paperback $9.95
LET'S US GO DOWN TO THE RIVER 'N...
        by Various Authors . . . . .paperback $9.95
LOST & BURIED TREASURE OF THE MISSOURI RIVER
        by Netha Bell . . . . .paperback $9.95
101 WAYS TO USE A DEAD RIVER FLY
        by Bruce Carlson . . . . .paperback $7.95
VACANT LOT, SCHOOL YARD & BACK ALLEY GAMES
        by Various Authors . . . . .paperback $9.95
HOW TO TALK MIDWESTERN
        by Robert Thomas . . . . .paperback $7.95

KENTUCKY BOOKS

TALES OF HACKETT'S CREEK
        by Dan Titus . . . . .paperback $9.95
LOST & BURIED TREASURE OF THE MISSISSIPPI RIVER
        by Netha Bell & Gary Scholl . . . . .paperback $9.95
LET'S US GO DOWN TO THE RIVER 'N...
        by Various Authors . . . . .paperback $9.95

101 WAYS TO USE A DEAD RIVER FLY
    by Bruce Carlson ....paperback $7.95
TALL TALES OF THE MISSISSIPPI RIVER
    by Dan Titus ....paperback $9.95
MY VERY FIRST
    by Various Authors ....paperback $9.95
VACANT LOT, SCHOOL YARD & BACK ALLEY GAMES
    by Various Authors ....paperback $9.95

MICHIGAN BOOKS

MICHIGAN COOKIN'
    by Bruce Carlson ....paperback $7.95
MICHIGAN'S ROADKILL COOKBOOK
    by Bruce Carlson ....paperback $7.95
MICHIGAN'S VANISHING OUTHOUSE
    by Bruce Carlson ....paperback $9.95

MINNESOTA BOOKS

MINNESOTA'S ROADKILL COOKBOOK
    by Bruce Carlson ....paperback $7.95
REVENGE OF ROADKILL
    by Bruce Carlson ....paperback $7.95
GHOSTS OF THE MISSISSIPPI RIVER
(from Minneapolis to Dubuque)
    by Bruce Carlson ....paperback $9.95
LAKES COUNTRY COOKBOOK
    by Bruce Carlson ....paperback $11.95

TALES OF HACKETT'S CREEK
     by Dan Titus . . . . .paperback $9.95
MINNESOTA'S VANISHING OUTHOUSE
     by Bruce Carlson . . . . .paperback $9.95
TALL TALES OF THE MISSISSIPPI RIVER
     by Dan Titus . . . . .paperback $9.95
Some Pretty Tame, but Kinda Funny Stories About Early
MINNESOTA LADIES-OF-THE-EVENING
     by Bruce Carlson . . . . .paperback $9.95
101 WAYS TO USE A DEAD RIVER FLY
     by Bruce Carlson . . . . .paperback $7.95
LOST & BURIED TEASURE OF THE MISSISSIPPI RIVER
     by Netha Bell & Gary Scholl . . . . .paperback $9.95
VACANT LOT, SCHOOL YARD & BACK ALLEY GAMES
     by Various Authors . . . . .paperback $9.95
HOW TO TALK MIDWESTERN
     by Robert Thomas . . . . .paperback $7.95
MINNESOTA COOKIN'
     by Bruce Carlson . . . .(3x5) paperback $5.95

MISSOURI BOOKS

MISSOURI COOKIN'
     by Bruce Carlson . . . .(3x5) paperback $5.95
MISSOURI'S ROADKILL COOKBOOK
     by Bruce Carlson . . . . .paperback $7.95
REVENGE OF THE ROADKILL
     by Bruce Carlson . . . . .paperback $7.95
LET'S US GO DOWN TO THE RIVER 'N...
     by Various Authors . . . . .paperback $9.95

LAKES COUNTRY COOKBOOK
          by Bruce Carlson ....paperback $11.95
101 WAYS TO USE A DEAD RIVER FLY
          by Bruce Carlson ....paperback $7.95
TALL TALES OF THE MISSISSIPPI RIVER
          by Dan Titus ....paperback $9.95
TALES OF HACKETT'S CREEK
          by Dan Titus ....paperback $9.95
STRANGE FOLKS ALONG THE MISSISSIPPI
          by Pat Wallace ....paperback $9.95
LOST AND BURIED TREASURE OF THE MISSOURI RIVER
          by Netha Bell ....paperback $9.95
HOW TO TALK MISSOURIAN
          by Bruce Carlson ....paperback $7.95
VACANT LOT, SCHOOL YARD & BACK ALLEY GAMES
          by Various Authors ....paperback $9.95
HOW TO TALK MIDWESTERN
          by Robert Thomas ....paperback $7.95
LOST & BURIED TREASURE OF THE MISSISSIPPI RIVER
          by Netha Bell & Gary Scholl ....paperback $9.95
MISSISSIPPI RIVER PO' FOLK
          by Pat Wallace ....paperback $9.95
Some Pretty Tame, but Kinda Funny Stories About Early
MISSOURI LADIES-OF-THE-EVENING
          by Bruce Carlson ....paperback $9.95
A FIELD GUIDE TO MISSOURI'S CRITTERS
          by Bruce Carlson ....paperback $7.95
EARLY MISSOURI HOME REMEDIES
          by Various Authors ....paperback $9.95
UNDERGROUND MISSOURI
          by Bruce Carlson ....paperpback $9.95
MISSISSIPPI RIVER COOKIN' BOOK
          by Bruce Carlson ....paperback $11.95

NEBRASKA BOOKS

LOST & BURIED TREASURE OF THE MISSOURI RIVER
  by Netha Bell .... paperback $9.95
101 WAYS TO USE A DEAD RIVER FLY
  by Bruce Carlson .... paperback $7.95
LET'S US GO DOWN TO THE RIVER 'N...
  by Various Authors .... paperback $9.95
HOW TO TALK MIDWESTERN
  by Robert Thomas .... paperback $7.95
VACANT LOT, SCHOOL YARD & BACK ALLEY GAMES
  by Various Authors .... paperback $9.95

TENNESSEE BOOKS

TALES OF HACKETT'S CREEK
  by Dan Titus .... paperback $9.95
TALL TALES OF THE MISSISSIPPI RIVER
  by Dan Titus .... paperback $9.95
UNSOLVED MYSTERIES OF THE MISSISSIPPI
  by Netha Bell .... paperback $9.95
LOST & BURIED TREASURE OF THE MISSISSIPPI RIVER
  by Netha Bell & Gary Scholl .... paperback $9.95
LET'S US GO DOWN TO THE RIVER 'N...
  by Various Authors .... paperback $9.95
101 WAYS TO USE A DEAD RIVER FLY
  by Bruce Carlson .... paperback $7.95
VACANT LOT, SCHOOL YARD & BACK ALLEY GAMES
  by Various Authors .... paperback $9.95

WISCONSIN

HOW TO TALK WISCONSIN . . . . .paperback $7.95
WISCONSIN COOKIN'
      by Bruce Carlson . . . .(3x5) paperback $5.95
WISCONSIN'S ROADKILL COOKBOOK
      by Bruce Carlson . . . . .paperback $7.95
REVENGE OF ROADKILL
      by Bruce Carlson . . . . .paperback $7.95
TALL TALES OF THE MISSISSIPPI RIVER
      by Dan Titus .paperback $9.95
LAKES COUNTRY COOKBOOK
      by Bruce Carlson . . . . .paperback $11.95
TALES OF HACKETT'S CREEK
      by Dan Titus .paperback $9.95
LET'S US GO DOWN TO THE RIVER 'N...
      by Various Authors . . . . .paperback $9.95
101 WAYS TO USE A DEAD RIVER FLY
      by Bruce Carlson . . . . .paperback $7.95
LOST & BURIED TREASURE OF THE MISSISSIPPI RIVER
      by Netha Bell & Gary Scholl . . . . .paperback $9.95
HOW TO TALK MIDWESTERN
      by Robert Thomas . . . . .paperback $7.95
VACANT LOT, SCHOOL YARD & BACK ALLEY GAMES
      by Various Authors . . . . .paperback $9.95
MY VERY FIRST
      by Various Authors . . . . .paperback $9.95
EARLY WISCONSIN HOME REMEDIES
      by Various Authors . . . . .paperback $9.95
THE VANISHING OUTHOUSE OF WISCONSIN
      by Bruce Carlson . . . . .paperback $9.95
GHOSTS OF DOOR COUNTY, WISCONSIN
      by Geri Rider . . . . .paperback $9.95

RIVER BOOKS

ON THE SHOULDERS OF A GIANT
by M. Cody and D. Walker . . . . .paperback $9.95
SKUNK RIVER ANTHOLOGY
by Gene "Will" Olson . . . . .paperback $9.95
JACK KING vs DETECTIVE MACKENZIE
by Netha Bell .paperback $9.95
LOST & BURIED TREASURE OF THE MISSISSIPPI RIVER
by Netha Bell & Gary Scholl . . . . .paperback $9.95
MISSISSIPPI RIVER PO' FOLK
by Pat Wallace . . . . .paperback $9.95
STRANGE FOLKS ALONG THE MISSISSIPPI
by Pat Wallace . . . . .paperback $9.95
TALES OF HACKETT'S CREEK
(1940s Mississippi River kids)
by Dan Titus . . . . .paperback $9.95
101 WAYS TO USE A DEAD RIVER FLY
by Bruce Carlson . . . . .paperback $7.95
LET'S US GO DOWN TO THE RIVER 'N...
by Various Authors . . . . .paperback $9.95
LOST & BURIED TREASURE OF THE MISSOURI
by Netha Bell .paperback $9.95
LIL' RED BOOK OF FISHING TIPS
by Tom Hollatz . . . . .paperback $7.95

COOKBOOKS

THE BACK-TO-THE SUPPER TABLE COOKBOOK
by Susie Babbington . . . . .paperback $11.95
THE COVERED BRIDGES COOKBOOK
by Bruce Carlson . . . . .paperback $11.95
COUNTRY COOKING-RECIPES OF MY AMISH HERITAGE
by Kathy Yoder . . . . .paperback $9.95
CIVIL WAR COOKIN', STORIES, 'N SUCH
by Darlene Funkhouser . . . . .paperback $9.95

SOUTHERN HOMEMADE
        by Lorraine Lott . . . . .paperback $11.95
THE ORCHARD, BERRY PATCHES, AND GARDEN CKBK
        by Bruce Carlson . . . . .paperback $11.95
THE BODY SHOP COOKBOOK
        by Sherrill Wolff . . . . .paperback $14.95
CAMP COOKING COOKBOOK
        by Mary Ann Kerl . . . . .paperback $9.95
FARMERS' MARKET COOKBOOK
        by Bruce Carlson . . . . .paperback $9.95
HERBAL COOKERY
        by Dixie Stephen . . . . .paperback $9.95
MAD ABOUT GARLIC
        by Pat Reppert . . . . .paperback $9.95
BREADS! BREADS! BREADS!
        by Mary Ann Kerl . . . . .paperback $9.95
PUMPKIN PATCHES, PROVERBS & PIES
        by Cherie Reilly . . . . .paperback $9.95
ARIZONA COOKING
        by Barbara Soden . . . . .paperback $5.95
SOUTHWEST COOKING
        by Barbara Soden . . . . .paperback $5.95
EATIN' OHIO
        by Rus Pishnery . . . . .paperback $9.95
EATIN' ILLINOIS
        by Rus Pishnery . . . . .paperback $9.95
KENTUCKY COOKIN'
        by Marilyn Carlson . . . . .paperback $5.95
INDIANA COOKIN'
        by Bruce Carlson . . . . .paperback $5.95
KANSAS COOKIN'
        by Bruce Carlson . . . . .paperback $5.95

NEW JERSEY COOKING
       by Bruce Carlson ....paperback $5.95
NEW MEXICO COOKING
       by Barbara Soden ....paperback $5.95
NEW YORK COOKIN'
       by Bruce Carlson ....paperback $5.95
OHIO COOKIN'
       by Bruce Carlson ....paperback $5.95
PENNSYLVANIA COOKING
       by Bruce Carlson ....paperback $5.95
AMISH-MENNONITE STRAWBERRY COOKBOOK
       by Alta Kauffman ....paperback $5.95
APPLES! APPLES! APPLES!
       by Melissa Mosley ....paperback $5.95
APPLES GALORE!!!
       by Bruce Carlson ....paperback $5.95
BERRIES! BERRIES! BERRIES!
       by Melissa Mosley ....paperback $5.95
BERRIES GALORE!!!
       by Bruce Carlson ....paperback $5.95
CHERRIES! CHERRIES! CHERRIES!
       by Marilyn Carlson ....paperback $5.95
CITRUS! CITRUS! CITRUS!
       by Lisa Nafziger ....paperback $5.95
COOKING WITH CIDER
       by Bruce Carlson ....paperback $5.95
COOKING WITH THINGS THAT GO BAA
       by Bruce Carlson ....paperback $5.95
COOKING WITH THINGS THAT GO CLUCK
       by Bruce Carlson ....paperback $5.95
COOKING WITH THINGS THAT GO OINK
       by Bruce Carlson ....paperback $5.95
GARLIC! GARLIC! GARLIC!
       by Bruce Carlson ....paperback $5.95

KID COOKIN'

        by Bev Faaborg . . . . .paperback $5.95

THE KID'S GARDEN FUN BOOK

        by Theresa McKeown . . . . .paperback $5.95

KID'S PUMPKIN FUN BOOK

        by J. Ballhagen . . . . .paperback $5.95

NUTS! NUTS! NUTS!

        by Melissa Mosley . . . . .paperback $5.95

PEACHES! PEACHES! PEACHES!

        by Melissa Mosley . . . . .paperback $5.95

PUMPKINS! PUMPKINS! PUMPKINS!

        by Melissa Mosley . . . . .paperback $5.95

VEGGIE-FRUIT-NUT MUFFIN RECIPES

        by Darlene Funkhouser . . . . .paperback $5.95

WORKING GIRL COOKING

        by Bruce Carlson . . . . .paperback $5.95

SOME LIKE IT HOT!!!

        by Barbara Soden . . . . .paperback $5.95

HOW TO COOK SALSA

        by Barbara Soden . . . . .paperback $5.95

COOKING WITH FRESH HERBS

        by Eleanor Wagner . . . . .paperback $5.95

BUFFALO COOKING

        by Momfeather . . . . .paperback $5.95

NO STOVE-NO SHARP KNIFE KIDS NO-COOK COOKBOOK

        by Timmy Denning . . . . .paperback $9.95

MISCELLANEOUS

HALLOWEEN
>by Bruce Carlson ....paperback $9.95

VEGGIE TALK
>by Glynn Singleton ....paperback $6.95

WASHASHORE
>by Margaret Potter ....paperback $9.95

PRINCES AND TOADS
>by Dr. Sharon Tobler ....paperback $12.95

HOW SOON CAN YOU GET HERE, DOC?
>by David Wynia, DVM ....paperback $9.95

MY PAW WAS A GREAT DANE
>by R. E. Rasmussen, DVM ....paperback $14.95

To order any of these books
from Quixote Press
call
1-800-571-2665